# LET MY PEOPLE KNOW!

## THE STORY
## OF
## ISSAC AND PATRICIA HALALI

## AS TOLD TO
## SUSAN K. REIDEL

# GOD'S PROMISE OVER JERUSALEM

THE ONLY CITY WHERE GOD CHOSE TO PUT HIS
NAME

# LET MY PEOPLE KNOW!

## THE STORY
## OF
## ISSAC AND PATRICIA HALALI

### AS TOLD TO
### SUSAN K. REIDEL

LOGOS TO RHEMA PUBLISHING/SUSAN K. REIDEL
4313 W. ELGIN STREET
BROKEN ARROW, OK 74012
Halali@sbcglobal.net

3

## COPYRIGHT

## DEDICATION

I want to dedicate this book, of my life, to my precious Mother-in-law, Mama Winnie, who is now in Heaven. She gave me my two best gifts. First, she gave me Yeshua and next she gave me her beautiful daughter, Patricia.

This completely changed my life. I became a whole and complete "ONE NEW MAN."

**MAMA WINNIE AND PATRICIA**

# THANKS

Each one listed below has had a part of our Heavenly Father's knowledge to impart in us. We have been blessed and have great love and gratitude for all of you. There are many more in our hearts and may God reward you for your service you gave so freely.

Dr. Robert and Margaret Lindsey (Israel)
Dr. Brad and Gayle Young (Israel and USA)
Prof. Lenore (Lindsey) and Ken Millican (Israel and USA)
Rabbi Curt and Christie Landry "House of David" with Pastors Tim and Sandy Alsbrough
Reverend George and Brenda Shafer
Pastor Larry and Linda Bishop (Dove Ministries)
Deborah Sweetin Evangelist and Television Host with "Battle Cry Ministries" with Robert Tucker
Reverend's Paul and Linda Nix
Rabbi Avraham and Dr. Irmeli Liberties
Reverend Robert Easton
Steve and Lila Tremble
Joan Bomholt (dear friend)
Judaic Artist Linda Martileno-Newton
Judaic Teacher Sally Bianca "One New Man Ministries"
Cynthia Ward and Louise Amick Ministers of "Hallelujah Women and Hallelujah Men"
Dennis and Rita Chambers with "Watchmen"
Pastors Fred and Linda West of Sukkat Chaim along with Associate Pastors Byron and Jimmie Kay Drywater "Torah Teachers"
Doug and Gloria Rachele
A special thank you to Susan K. Reidel for your God given talents and your patience (solve-la-nute) in hours spent writing this book.

# TABLE OF CONTENTS

There is an old saying, "Life is hard," but I would add to that, "Life is harder in Israel."

This book is the life story of Issac and Patricia Halali. As I did my research and interviews I came to know a man and woman that were chosen by Almighty God. Issac was gifted in art and iron works, for the purpose and plans God had for Israel and His Church.

Issac was born in the Old City of Jerusalem and fought in the Suez War, 1956, The Six Day War, 1967, and The Yom Kippur War, 1973.

His wife Pat stands with him in their life's work. In the book of Exodus 31:1-11, there is the story of Bezalel and Oholiab, *"...men that were filled with the Spirit of God with wisdom, with understanding, with knowledge and with all kinds of skill; to make artistic designs for work in gold, silver and bronze, to cut and set stones, to work in wood, and to engage in all kinds of crafts."*

*Exodus 31:1-11*

*"And the LORD spake unto Moses, saying,*

*2 See, I have called by name Bezaleel the son of Uri, the son of Hur, of the tribe of Judah:*

*3 And I have filled him with the spirit of God, in wisdom, and in understanding, and in knowledge, and in all manner of workmanship,*

*⁴ To devise cunning works, to work in gold, and in silver, and in brass,*

*⁵ And in cutting of stones, to set them, and in carving of timber, to work in all manner of workmanship.*

*⁶ And I, behold, I have given with him Aholiab, the son of Ahisamach, of the tribe of Dan: and in the hearts of all that are wise hearted I have put wisdom, that they may make all that I have commanded thee;*

*⁷ The tabernacle of the congregation, and the ark of the testimony, and the mercy seat that is thereupon, and all the furniture of the tabernacle,*

*⁸ And the table and his furniture, and the pure candlestick with all his furniture, and the altar of incense,*

*⁹ And the altar of burnt offering with all his furniture, and the laver and his foot,*

*¹⁰ And the cloths of service, and the holy garments for Aaron the priest, and the garments of his sons, to minister in the priest's office,*

*¹¹ And the anointing oil, and sweet incense for the holy place: according to all that I have commanded thee shall they do."*

Issac is just such a man. He built from architectural plans the gates of the Presidential Palace in Israel. His workmanship is known internationally and his life is a fascinating read for anyone! I believe the reader of this book will come to the end and give honor to God, this man and his wife, where honor is due. It is rare in this lifetime that you get to meet such incredible people with the life story they have.

When I read the Exodus verse I saw all the pieces designed and developed for the Tabernacle. These Spirit-filled artists laid the foundation, structure, and instruments to worship God in the Tabernacle.

Today, in Yeshua, we are that Temple and the Spirit of God resides in us. Issac through his exceptional artistic abilities shows us how to do the same. He is under a command and assignment of God to create the blending of the Jewish foundations with the grace of Yeshua, to create the beauty of the Lord in each one of us, as God's created masterpiece, through his works of art.

Usually publishers don't write forwards, but I had to fulfill Jeremiah 30:2 as I got to know and understand this prophetic artist of God.

*Jeremiah 30:2*

*"This is the word that came to Jeremiah from the Lord: "*
*This is what the Lord, the God of Israel, says: 'Write in a*
*book all the words I have spoken to you.*

11

I believe this book is a divine assignment for me to write, but greater still for the blessing that will come to the reader! Find a comfortable chair and a quiet place and begin your journey into the life of a man who will show God's grace to you, through God's grace to him. An incredible and fascinating story of a man whom God has touched and blessed for His glory!

Publisher/Writer Susan K.

PRESIDENT'S PALACE GATE 1969

# CROSS CREATED FOR DOVE CHURCH

## IN

## JENKS, OKLAHOMA

Issac and Pat attend Dove Church in Jenks, OK.
The Pastors are Larry and Linda Bishop, 'gifts' in
The Kingdom of God!

PATRICIA AND ISSAC HALALI

Issac and Menorah

# CHAPTER ONE

# HAVE YOU EVER BEEN HUNGRY?

೪ುೞ

War is a horrible thing to endure! In 1948 Issac was right in the middle of it. Having been born in the Old City of Jerusalem, and the oldest of all his brothers and sisters. As a thirteen year old boy, he came to know the sacrifices of war. With nine brothers and sisters, he was the oldest of ten children. He had great responsibilities. In the early morning hours bombs would streak through the sky and drop on Jerusalem, his home city. There was a great deal of fear and stress, but as a thirteen year old boy he had to grow up quickly. In the early morning hours Issac would run out into the city, dodging bombs, to get to the fields where he would gather grass for food to help feed his family. Issac attended Bet Arron School (House of Arron) for nine years from the age of five, and endured the hunger, bombs, and fears of a childhood growing up in Israel. He would have to be successful daily or his brothers and sisters would continue to feel the pangs of hunger. An empty stomach with no way to fill it was not an option for Issac to even consider. He knew what he had to do and he faced his fears head on. He collected grass to bring home so his mother could fry it and feed all her children. Also, there was a horse that carried tanks of water that would come into the town and Issac would stand in line, waiting to fill his container for the family needs. He did this every time the horse came. You could not afford to miss getting the water your family was in desperate need of.

Childhood was hard, but becoming a man harder. When Issac was thirteen years old it was time for his Bar-Mitzvah. It was also 1948, and Israel had just become a new nation recognized by the world. War started immediately and because of bomb raids daily Issac didn't get to celebrate and have presents. It was time for war responsibilities to help protect the family. It was not a party time and Issac had already picked up the responsibilities of a man!

It seemed like the greatest challenge and mission of his young life was to find food and water! Food became a major issue for this large family. He recounts a story of how his father would take Issac and his brother Shaul to synagogue and tell his mother, who had been cooking what little they had, to turn off the heat on everything while they were gone. Mother didn't want to do that because she wanted the children to have warm food. This seemed to be a serious matter of discussion and constant reminding for Sabbath practice.

Years later his sister told Issac she was the lookout to tell when father was on the way back from synagogue. Upon their return they would take their places at the table and be served warm food! Issac's father would tell them, "See I told you God is taking care of us with warm food."

He would be so grateful, but as a boy he wondered where and how this warm food was coming to them. One day his mother saw his questioning and pulled him aside. She made him vow not to tell his father, to which he agreed. "Well every time you left the house for synagogue I would turn the heat back on!" This showed Issac, for the first time, how different his mother and father were in their thinking. Issac's mother was more liberal with the Scriptures. His father was conservative and Orthodox, and he believed they had to do every little thing in the Torah or God would punish them. He wanted his family to be honorable and obedient. This put a real scare into Issac that if he did something wrong he would be punished by God.

It was hard for Issac, but times were hard. One thing he knew for sure was that his father loved his family and Issac loved him. This was who he was and his father's sternness was his way of showing what he believed, and his willingness to obey and expect his children to honor and respect God is how he lived.

In fact, he wanted Issac to be a Rabbi and wanted to send him to a Yeshiva (special school), Issac went to Beth Aaron School. One incident Issac recalled, that showed an incredible love from his father for him, was when Issac was seven years old. He was leaving school and an Arab, riding a motorcycle, tried to run Issac over.

"He hit me and I broke my ankle bone. I was writhing in pain, but to my surprise my father showed up!" He was there. Issac was so surprised he was there at the right time! He picked Issac up and carried him all the way home. When they got home his mother and father tried to fix Issac up. They did not know that his foot was broken. The pain was unbearable and this went on for three months. No one knew what else to do for Issac. At this time they did not have pain pills to help him, but Issac states, "I can say my father stayed with me, all night and would tell me stories to take my mind off the pain." It was a profound pain to endure, but the way Issac came to know his father was a real blessing.

Finally, it was obvious something major was wrong and they took Issac to the Anglican Hospital where it was made known that he had broken his bone. A cast and setting was done to help with the healing process. As painful as this experience was in his life he also realized it is one of his fondest memories of his father's love for him. "We were not rich in this world's goods, but we were rich in love." This was a bitter but sweet memory of his father's love for his son. Later as Issac grew into a young man he would learn of a greater Father's love for His Son, Yeshua, and Issac would come to know healing in a divine and purposeful way.

In 1948 Israel became a nation and war broke out immediately. It was a very happy time because Israel was now a Jewish Nation and at the same time the worst of all things with no army and no real time to solidify their independence.

War broke out. The war of 1948, was to hold on to the Independence Israel had just been given. It was truly a miracle of God that saved Israel with no standing army, no economy to fund the war effort, and a population not trained to fight a mobilized and supplied enemies!

Again, Issac would know real hunger. There was very little food and Israel had to feed the men and women who were fighting to save Israel. The nation was given rations of one half of a loaf of bread to each of the families. Food was scarce and not only did you have to sacrifice to keep your family alive you now had to help keep the fighting soldiers supplied. This was not a chore to Issac, it was a privilege he was more than willing to sacrifice for it.

Issac's mother sent him on a food mission once again. He was to go to a little grocery store to pick up their ration of bread. He went to the store and picked up the one-half of the bread loaf to help feed his brothers and sisters. He recounts what happened next. "I picked up the one-half-loaf of bread and was so hungry, I ate half of it! I felt bad, guilty, and ashamed, but I couldn't help it I was starving and never knew hunger pain like that!" He was only thirteen years old. When he got home he gave what was left to his mother. She looked at it and then at Issac. She said, "What have you done son?" A question that even today when thought about brings such hurt to his heart. "This is for the family and you ate half of it?"

The next thing he knew was that she did not punish him, but she hugged him! He will never forget that gesture of compassion. Hunger pain is about the worst thing you can feel. Hunger suffering can make you do things you would never think you could do, but it is something he will never forget. He also will never forget that hug of forgiveness from his mother. Her compassion for his sorrow was greater than he had ever felt. He knew in his whole being he deserved to be punished severely, but his mother gave him forgiveness freely. It is only all these years later Issac realized her compassion came out because she was experiencing that same hunger, but having the added knowledge her children were suffering too.

Later, Issac was to learn this same mercy and grace when he accepted Yeshua as his Messiah. Yeshua had done the same unconditional love for him.

So I ask you, "Have you ever been hungry?"

ISSAC'S FATHER AND MOTHER

ABRAHAM HALALI AND MARGOLITH HALALI

HORSE USED FOR WATER TANK

# CHAPTER TWO

# WAR THE COMMON THREAD OF ISRAEL

৪০৫৪

W ar is the tear drops of every nation. It breaks the heart and spirit of its people and even when victory comes the price paid for it cannot be summed up. It was difficult to raise ten siblings, but Issac's father and mother did it, and did it with great commitment and love. Every day Issac's father would walk him and Shaul to the synagogue at sunrise to pray. He would do this when Issac was around four years old to fourteen years old. That took commitment and a great faith. Issac learned much about a strong work ethic and about a strong faith through watching his father and holding him in great respect.

Problems had started to escalate between the Arabs and Jews so the family decided to leave their synagogue and home and make a major move. When Issac was five one day his father told him they were moving out of the Old City and Issac cried at that news. This was heart wrenching for Issac. This was his only place he felt safe in, now it would be gone too. To comfort Issac his father told him, "One day you will be back." Issac took those words deep into his heart and knew they were true and would come to pass someday. He waited and hoped for that day. This became the longing of his heart.

By 1942, Issac was seven years old, the Nazi's were in Egypt, and Issac's school told them when they came to school to bring a knife and try to kill one German before they kill you! Because of the tough times at his Bar-Mitzvah Issac did not receive any presents. It seemed like a childhood was out of the question for Issac. The time when young men play and enjoy their days was not a possibility for Issac.

The war started when the British left the area, after the UN voted for Israel to have a small piece of land for a Jewish state. In 1948, the United Nations voted to let Israel become a nation for the Jewish people. At the time when young Issac was turning thirteen bombs were going off all the time! Bombs were common to Issac and it was a situation that was scary, but something he had to face and endure. There was nowhere to run and hide, yet Issac sensed God's providence in his life even at a young age. Issac's father, Abraham Halali, and his mother, Margolith Halali, had moved from the Old City in Jerusalem to the outskirts of the Old City in the Jewish Quarter.

Moving to the outside of Jerusalem to the area of Mahane Yehuda by the Shuk Market was not easy. The Shuk Market was an open air space where vendors sold fresh fruits and vegetables; baked goods; fish, meat and cheeses; nuts, seeds, and spices; clothing and shoes; and housewares.

During the Ottoman rule, the market expanded and sanitary conditions worsened. By the 1920s, the British Mandate authorities cleared out all the merchants and built permanent stalls and roofing. Afterwards, the market began to be known as the Mahane Yehuda Market, after the larger neighborhood. 1. Having a very large family this just seemed like the place they needed to be.

1..Rosenthal, Morris (May 2009). "Mahane Yehuda – The Jerusalem Shuk (Outdoor Market)". Foner Books.com. Retrieved June 17, 2010

The Arabs would not let any food trucks make it into Jerusalem, but ambushed and killed all and anyone that tried. This went on for about one and a half years. Issac's mother would send him out to find and get certain grass to fix for all his brothers and sisters to eat. It was dangerous and yet had to be done, if they were going to survive. Each family was rationed a little water every few days. The trucks were prevented from coming into the area and hunger was something men, women, and children felt every day. It was miserable and very discouraging, but everyone was willing to sacrifice for their nation, Israel. Everyone was willing to sacrifice for the promise to return Israel out of her captivity back to the Promised Land!

One day a potato truck finally made it through into his family's area and there was great excitement. A classmate of Issac jumped to get a potato from the truck and slipped. He fell under the truck and was killed. This was heartbreaking and a memory of the hard times Issac and his family lived through. Issac had to accept the cruelties of war, but he did everything he could to protect his family, friends, and country.

Finally, the Israelis got a different road built, the Berma Road, to get through from Tel Aviv to Jerusalem. This road was used to bring in supplies. The burnt out food trucks, that were attacked, are still on the side of the road as a remembrance to those who sacrificed their lives to bring food to the families. This road was going to allow "food" to come into town and ease the hunger situation for a while.

Life in Israel was tough for a teen like Issac, but he had many responsibilities with all his brothers and sisters. It was expected of him and he carried it heavy in his heart and wanted to do his best. Hunger is one of the conditions of war that everyone experiences and it is heartbreaking. Many nights Issac and his friends would sneak out and put up banners and signs to try and get the British to leave Israel because they allowed the Arabs to arm themselves, but not the Jewish people. This was a very dangerous thing to do and if caught could have led to his and his friends deaths. They wanted to do all they could and they took great risks.

War is a constant, or shall I say a constant conflict is always taking place in Israel. In 1953, Issac went into the military for two and a half years. This is the expected service for all men and girls to go into the military service to do their part. It is a time of separation from the family. A time you worry about your absence and if will hurt the family. Yet, you feel pride and character to be able to go into the service and serve for the greater good in Israel. Men and women serve in active service for two and a half years and serve one month a year until age fifty-five. The women serve two years, but if they are married they don't serve in the army anymore. They must also be ready to go back to service should the need arise.

That need came again in 1956 when the Suez Canal War began. Egyptian President Gamal Abdel Nasser took control of the Suez Canal and nationalized it. He was provoking the Western World and humiliating them by taking their control away. Egypt loathed Israel! It was feared they would cut off Israeli ships and so Israel struck first. In two days the British and the French joined them in the battle to regain the canal.

Eventually, Russia and the United States were involved enough to cause a withdrawal of British, French, and Israeli military, after the canal was recaptured Issac realized with many other young men that they had stood up to defend the nation of Israel's interest. After the Suez War Britain and France lost a lot of their influence as leaders in the world. Israel was standing even stronger in the eyes of the world. Issac was proud and realized that Israel and its people were his heartbeat and purpose.

It is hard for those not born or who haven't lived in Israel to understand, but you must believe God has a plan for your life, and He will bring you down the paths you must travel to get there. Trust God has a plan for your life.

JEWISH SAYING AND BELIEF

BURNING BUSH "LET MY PROPLE GO!"
IN HEBREW 18" WIDE X 24" HIGH

CHAPTER THREE

## BECOMING AN ARTIST FOR ISRAEL

&ເນC8

O nce again war had come and gone and Issac was about to enter into the purpose for his life. When Issac was fourteen his father told him it was time for him to go to work to help the family financially and to be able to go to school at night. Issac knew in his heart that he wanted to create things and not to sit in an office. Issac went to work with Moshe Shapiro a well-known, skilled, welder from Poland and began to apprentice under his mentoring. Shapiro's family were blacksmiths and he was famous for his art. This was a tremendous opportunity for Issac.

Issac settled in well with his apprenticeship and worked for Sharipo for three and a half years. In 1958 one month before Independence Day, the government asked Shapiro to make hundreds of "The Lion of Judah," on the Jerusalem flag, out of metal, to put on every light post for the ten year statehood celebration. Sharipo and Issac worked day and night with only two to three hours of sleep a day to accomplish this celebration of Israel's memorial piece. Israel was now ten years old and Issac was a part of representing the strength of Israel by being a part of making these memorial pieces that were put on the lamp posts of Israel. This was a great honor and an enormous accomplishment for Issac and Sharipo. Issac could see that God was blessing the country he struggled in, defended, and loved through this artwork he was producing with his famous mentor.

31

Matthew 5:16
*"In the same way, let your light
shine before men, so that they may see your good works and
give glory to your Father in heaven."*

It was in the heart of Issac to let the light of Yeshua shine through him, to others in kindness and love, and his gift artistically. Every light post with "The Lion of Judah" was showing all of Israel that all the sacrifices they had made were being represented in this "good work" and all the people could celebrate with rejoicing for God had kept Israel as the "Apple of His Eye." Issac felt great pride and honor for the part he had in this "good work."

In 1959, Issac decided to open his own shop so Sharipo helped Issac fulfill a dream to own and operate his own shop. In the 60's the business was doing very well and once again Issac was called back to military service one month before the Six-Day War began. No one knew how long the war would last. The government wanted hooks welded on all tractors and trailers to be able to pull weapons, supplies, people, and whatever was needed for the war effort.

All Arab countries came together against Israel. It was about 70 million Arabs against 500,000 Israelis! Also, tanks and airplanes outnumbered Israel forces 100 to 1. Incredible opposition! Impossible odds, but Issac and the Israeli people had experienced the miracles of God and believed somehow God would deliver again. Never-the-less, in real life, the odds were staggering against Israel! Israel decided to stage a preemptive air assault and destroyed more than ninety percent of Egypt's air force while they were still on the ground! They did the same with the Syrian air force! The Arabs were now extremely vulnerable.

32

In three days the Israelis had achieved overwhelming success and captured the Gaza Strip and Sinai Peninsula up to the east bank of the Suez Canal. Only God!

Now it was time to open the eastern front. The Jordanians expected the Israelis to attack at Jaffa Gate, of the Old City, but Issac and the ones with him went around in back to the Lion's Gate. The command car was too wide to go through so they knocked off part of the entrance with the command car. Israeli forces drove forces out of East Jerusalem and most of the West Bank. The Old City, Jerusalem, was now, finally back in the control of the Jewish nation!

The paratroopers had landed and attacked already and many of them were killed. There was sniper fire going on everywhere. It was dangerous, yet Issac felt so excited remembering what his father had told him about one day he would be back in the Old City!

Here he was at the Wailing Wall, Israel's army victorious. Touching the wall all he could do along with the others was cry like babies! The joy, excitement, and heartfelt emotions were unexplainable even to this day! This was a miracle of God and everyone realized 2,000 years of hope had just been fulfilled! Issac once again was in a prophetic assignment of God.

When Moshe Dayan and Chief Rabbi Slomo Goren were there the Rabbi blew the shofar and wanted Dayan to have the Mosque of Omar controlled by the Israelis, but Dayan would not do it. Actually, the Six Day War was really won in six hours! Israel's Air Force attacked Syria, Jordan, and Egypt's' planes, while they were all on the ground, and their air forces were almost completely destroyed by Israel!

33

One of the events that Issac remembers was on the way to the Sinai they saw thousands of boots in the sand. The Egyptians had taken off their boots when they became scared, and realized they could run faster with their boots off. When Issac saw the thousands of boots he wanted to collect them and open a shoe store!

Before going to the Sini Issac and his commander went to Jericho. On the way they saw an Arabic family with children walking with all they could carry on their backs. Issac had the car stop and asked the old man in Arabic where they were going? The man said they were trying to get to Jericho because the soldiers were coming to their village and would kill them. Issac told him they were already in Jericho and they were not going to kill anyone, except the enemy, who had the guns.

Issac gave them his water since it was a hot day and told them to go back to their village. He assured them that they would be safe. Issac had learned from the time he was a child what a piece of bread and a drink of water could mean to the soul so looking at this family he knew their greatest need was a drink of water and he freely gave it.

About a month later he went to their village to check on them and the whole village knew the story. They killed a lamb and made dinner for Issac and the old man gave Issac some shekels in appreciation. For a short moment in time there was peace. The prayer of two-thousand years, "Next year in Jerusalem" was a tremendous and joyous event. Issac was part of this moment in history as tears ran from his eyes happy to be alive and proud to see Jerusalem back as a part of the promise of God in the control of Israel. Truly a miracle!

The losses to the Arabs were disastrous about eighteen thousand Arabs were lost to Israel's only seven hundred! It truly was considered a miracle of Almighty God.

Issac was part of a giant prophetic moment in history. He was part of the fulfillment of Scripture and crying, dancing, and worshipping he had been part of the army to liberate Jerusalem and able to pray at the Wailing Wall. Issac came to knowing God is great! God is faithful, and his personal journey in God's plan for his life was exciting and wonderful to experience.

ISSAC'S FATHER AND UNCLE AT THE KOTEL
(WAILING WALL) ON THE FIRST DAY AFTER
ISRAEL TOOK BACK THE OLD CITY

HEAD RABBI SLOWMO GOREN 1967
WHEN THEY REACHED KOTEL

ISSAC AT 18 YEARS OLD

CHAPTER FOUR

# DO UNTO OTHERS...

ೞೞ

When life is hard you face many challenges. Many of the things that become hurtful, painful, and emotionally hard to handle, are not just the personal things you experience. Issac was not the only person struggling to stay alive in Israel. Everyone was basically in the same position of hardship. For almost two years daily requirements were hard to come by, but when the Burma Road was built every year got a little easier in the battle for survival. As Issac walked around the city and worked in his iron shop he saw people every day hungry and just trying to make it to the next day. He was determined to do whatever he could to help another person. Issac realized that others were struggling, some worse than he was. He kept a sensitive and open heart to help if he could.

One day while working he noticed an older woman trying to drag an old iron bed down the street. As he watched her struggle he noticed that one of the iron legs was broken. She pushed and pulled with all her strength, but to Issac it looked futile. Issac went out to see what he could do to help her.

He examined the situation and made the decision to weld the leg back on and fix it for her. As he worked on it he could see the worry in her face. He knew she didn't have any money to pay him. Issac could tell she was blessed to have the bed fixed. It was an act of compassion she fully understood and was grateful for it.

When he returned it to her she asked, "How much?" As she reached for her small weathered coin purse Issac just blurted out fifty shekels at which he thought she was going to faint. But at the same time he said it he reached into his pocket and pulled out fifty shekels and gave it to her! "You are paying me to fix my bed?"
"Yes," Issac said incredulously. It was a special moment and he realized he couldn't solve everyone's difficulties, but he could use the gifts God had given him to help others when he saw the need. Issac lived his life this way, "Do unto others what you would have others do unto you." Later while reading scriptures he came across the story of the Good Samaritan and he said to himself, "I'm a good Samaritan!" Issac always had a compassionate heart and has tried to live his life as a Good Samaritan.

Growing up in Israel especially before all the modern cities and conveniences were built was exciting and dangerous. War and having to go to battle was never out of Issac's young mind. He remembers being in the army and having a sergeant who was extremely hard on him. He would ask Issac to do things he just physically could not do. He disliked him and one day Issac had had enough. He demanded Issac do some crazy thing and Issac said to him, "No, I can't do it!"
"What do you mean C A N 'T!" The voice was booming.
"I mean I can't and I won't!"
Fury came up in his face and Issac knew he was probably going to prison. For some reason the sergeant decided to take him to the ole proverbial woodshed and duke it out with him.

The fight was on! Fist were swinging, feet were moving, and the thought of death or great pain was swirling in Issac's mind. When it was over somehow they were both standing and the most unusual outcome was experienced. They became good friends! Life had given Issac another twist of fate.

As a young man army life was lonely and many times he just wanted to go home. In fact, that's just what he did one time. Issac snuck out of camp and decided he wanted to see his family. He missed them and was worried about them. He wanted to make sure they were doing well so he made the decision to go find out on his own. He got himself into a very awkward situation with some guard dogs and although he didn't want to hurt them he had to shoot them because they were attacking him. After Issac came back into camp he had the good foresight to clean his weapon. Before the day was over the owners of the dogs came to the base to get to the bottom of the matter about their dogs. They checked everyone's guns and thankfully Issac's were cleaned so no fingers got pointed at him!

Army life was difficult, but no more so than daily existence for everyone. Even the enemy endured and questioned. Once Issac's commanding officer asked Issac to go with him to question the prisoners of war. Issac spoke Arabic well and he asked one Egyptian prisoner, when they found all the boots in the desert why they ran away from the battle? The Egyptian answered in a matter of fact way, "This is not my country! If it was my country we would stand and fight. Why should we die for this country it is not our home." Everyone in war questions the things they experience and endure. The enemy was no exception.

When Jerusalem was finally liberated Issac didn't think he had words to express what a wonder and amazing thing this was. Over two thousand years waiting to go into Jerusalem and finally at the Six Day War he found himself in a divine appointment of history. There are no words or emotions that can express what his heart and mind were feeling. Tears were coming from his eyes and he was part of prophetic history! Enemy soldiers were surrendering in masses. Israel and the whole world gradually began to realize the magnitude of the Israeli victory in a six-day war.

On the Egyptian front: 600 Egyptian tanks were destroyed and some 100 captured. 10,000 Egyptian soldiers were killed and more than 5,000 taken prisoner. Ground to air missiles containing gas containers was discovered never having been fired! The miracle of defeat was amazing and the world stood in awe of little Israel. God's hand was on Israel's army and Issac knew and realized once again he was part of a divine plan for his country.

The Western Wall was opened to the people of Israel and on June 14, 1967, on the day of Shavuot (the Jewish Pentecost) 200,000 visitors made their way to pray at the Wall, the first pilgrimage since the Dispersion! The emotions of hundreds of thousands was something Issac will never forget. He didn't realize when he broke off the piece of wall with his vehicle what a tremendous miracle was taking place.

Even today, as Issac makes his home in Tulsa, OK he still finds himself constantly longing to be back in Israel. He prays this is the year God makes the way for Patricia and him to return in His will. This sacred place is where their hearts will always be.

CAPTURING JERUSALEM BEFORE ON THE LEFT
AND AFTER ON THE RIGHT

ISRAEL WILL NEVER FORGET THE
WORDS OF MOTTA GUR, "THE TEMPLE
MOUNT IS OURS!"

BEFORE AND AFTER

# CHAPTER FIVE

# THE YOM KIPPUR WAR

ℰℭ

In 1973 The Yom Kippur War started and it was very bad. Many in the IDF were killed. Since this was one of the holiest days in Israel all the people were in the synagogues fasting and praying. There were no cars, radio, or TV. You could hear a pin drop in Israel on this day. At 10:00 a.m. Issac began to hear cars and turned on the radio. He heard his code to report and he did so. His younger brother had only been in the military for three weeks and was sent to the Golan Heights.

(The following article describes this war in detail.

---

This article was written by Gary Rashba and originally published in the October 1998 issue of *Military History* magazine.)

The Yom Kippur War and the Battle for The Golan Heights was a battle between Syrian and Israeli forces that took place at the beginning of the War. Syrian tanks vastly outnumbered Israeli tanks.

Defeat seemed to be imminent for the state of Israel. The Syrians' Soviet-style massive frontal assault was too much to bear, and the Israeli front lines had already collapsed. On October 6, 1973, during Yom Kippur, the holiest day of the Jewish calendar, a Syrian armored force of 1,400 tanks backed by more than 1,000 artillery pieces and supporting air power began a coordinated assault along the 36-mile-long Israeli-Syrian Syrian border in the Golan Heights in the north of Israel.

That attack coincided with a similar onslaught by Egyptian forces along the Suez Canal, suddenly forcing Israel to fight a two-front war.

Israeli defense doctrine relies on the standing army to hold the line with air support while the reserves are mobilized. Therefore, the two Israeli brigades that stood in the Syrians' way in the Golan had the daunting task of holding off the onslaught long enough for Israel's reserve mobilization to kick in. The 7th Armored Brigade's epic defense of the northern Golan has come to be widely regarded as one of the finest defensive stands in military history. Less publicity has been given to the heroism of the shattered fragments of the 188th (Barak) Brigade in slowing the Syrian advance in the south. In some respects, however, the Barak Brigade's story is more incredible, considering the fact that hundreds of Syrian tanks had overrun its sector and were held off by only a handful of Israeli tanks.

The 1973 conflict was as much about honor as it was about real estate. In the Six-Day War of June 1967, Israel had seized the Golan Heights, which Syria had turned into one large network of bunkers and artillery positions. For years, Syrian gunners, shooting at random and without provocation, would fire on Israeli fishermen plying their trade on the Sea of Galilee or at Israeli farmers in the Hula Valley below. In a costly uphill battle, the Israelis swept out the Syrian defenders and put an end to the harassment. The loss of the Golan Heights in 1967, however, had been humiliating to Syria.

Between 1967 and 1973, there were frequent skirmishes along the cease-fire line. For months leading up to its attack, the Syrian army had been fully mobilized and on war alert. Since the

Israelis were accustomed to seeing those forces at battle strength, the Syrians were able to make final attack preparations without sending noteworthy warning signals. Furthermore, with tensions escalating between the two countries, Israeli leadership feared that strengthening its defenses might be misconstrued as preparation for a pre-emptive strike, thus provoking the Syrians to attack.

The Golan Heights are made up of a 480-square-mile volcanic (basalt) rock plateau perched above the Hula Valley to the west and Jordan Valley to the south. It rises gently from 600 feet in the south to 3,000 feet in the north, with abrupt escarpments dominating the valleys to the west and south. It is transected in some areas by impassable canyons, limiting the number of routes leading up from the valleys to the heights. Since the heights' geography restricted defensive mobility, Israel continued its advance against the routed Syrians in 1967 until a defensible line was reached—a string of extinct volcano cones that commands strategic views of Damascus on one side and of all northern Israel on the other.

Israeli defenses were based on seventeen fortified observation posts. The Purple Line, as the 1967 cease-fire line was known, marked the end of the no man's land separating Syria from the Golan. Lacking a true defensive barrier, the Israelis had dug a twenty-mile-long anti-tank ditch along the border from Mount Hermon to Rafid, an obstacle Syrian armor would be forced to cross under fire from Israeli tanks positioned behind ramparts. At the outbreak of hostilities in 1973, the Golan Heights were defended by two armored brigades: the 7th, which had only been dispatched to the northern sector on October 4, and the 188th (Barak) Brigade, a regular fixture intimately familiar with the area's terrain, in the south. The modified Centurion and M-48 Patton tanks fielded by both brigades were fitted with the 105mm NATO gun and modern diesel engines.

Considering the faulty Israeli intelligence assessment that, at most, armed skirmishes with the Syrians would break out, the 170 tanks and 70 artillery pieces in the Golan were thought to be enough to meet any Syrian threats, at least until the reserves would arrive.

Against that comparatively small force, the Syrian army fielded five divisions for its attack: two armored and three mechanized infantry, including some 1,400 tanks. Approximately 400 of those tanks were T-62s, the most modern Soviet-bloc tank at the time, equipped with a 115mm smoothbore gun and infrared night-fighting capability. The balance were T-54s and T-55s armed with 100mm guns. The Syrian plan called for its 5th, 7th and 9th mechanized infantry divisions, in BTR-50 armored personnel carriers (APCs) supported by 900 tanks, to breach the Israeli lines, opening the way for the 1st and 3rd armored divisions to move in with their 500 tanks to capture the entire Golan Heights before Israel had a chance to mobilize.

At 2 p.m. on October 6, Syrian gunners opened up a tremendous barrage along the entire front as a prelude to their two-pronged attack–a northern one in the vicinity of the Kuneitra-Damascus road and one in the south where Rafid bulges into Syria.

Facing Colonel Avigdor Ben-Gal's 7th Armored Brigade in the Golan's northern sector were the Syrian 3rd Armored Division under Brig. Gen. Mustapha Sharba, the 7th Mechanized Infantry Division and the Assad Republican Guard. When the Syrian assault began, mine-clearing tanks and bridge-layers led the way to overcome the Israeli obstacles. Naturally, those engineering vehicles were the 7th's first targets, but Syrian infantrymen, braving intense fire from the heights, rushed forward and used their entrenching tools to build up enough earthen causeways for their tanks to negotiate the Israeli anti-tank ditches.

While the Israelis took out every Syrian vehicle they could get into their sights, the sheer mass of some 500 enemy tanks and 700 APCs advancing toward their lines ensured that the defenses would be overwhelmed. The number of defenders dwindled as Israeli tanks were knocked out, yet the vastly outnumbered Israelis managed to take a heavy toll on Syrian armor. In spite of their heavy losses, the Syrians pressed their attack without letup, yet the overexerted 7th managed to hold its ground, throwing stopgap blocking actions wherever the Syrians were on the verge of breaking through.

When darkness fell, the Israelis had nothing to match the Syrians' night-vision gear and had to allow the enemy armor to advance to ranges effective for night fighting. In the close fighting, the Syrians succeeded in seizing some of the high ground, but a counterattack by the small group of persistent defenders forced them back. When some Syrian tanks did overrun the Israeli lines, the 7th's gunners would rotate their turrets to destroy them and then immediately turn their attention back to other oncoming tanks. It amounted to an armored version of hand-to-hand combat.

The battle raged for two more days as the Syrians, seemingly oblivious to their heavy losses, continued their assault without letup. By the afternoon of October 9, the 7th Brigade was down to six tanks protecting what was for all intents and purposes a clear path into Israel's north.

Those last few tanks fought until they were down to their last rounds. Then, just as the 7th Brigade tanks were finally starting to pull back, they were suddenly augmented by an impromptu force of some 15 tanks. The Syrians believed the clock had run out and that the first of the fresh Israeli reservists had arrived, and the Syrian offensive ran out of steam.

In truth, it was a motley force of repaired tanks crewed by injured and other crewman, which had been mustered by Lt. Col. Yossi Ben-Hanan, a veteran commander who, upon hearing about the outbreak of war, had hurried home from his honeymoon overseas. By virtue of its timing, that force proved to be the 7th Brigade's saving grace.

As individual tanks began to augment the Israeli forces, the Syrians, exhausted from three days of continuous fighting and unaware of how close to victory they actually were, turned in retreat. Hundreds of destroyed tanks and APCs littering the valley below the Israeli ramparts were testimony to the horrible destruction that had taken place there, leading an Israeli colonel to dub it the 'Valley of Tears.'

Meanwhile, the Syrians, whose objectives included seizing the bridges spanning the Jordan River (most of which could be easily reached through the southern Golan), concentrated a large part of their attack in that sector. Up against hundreds of enemy tanks in a line of armor as far as the eye could see, the Barak Brigade crews had no choice but to hold fast, because the terrain did not allow for much defensive maneuvering. Retreat would give the Syrians nearly free reign to seize the entire heights and move on the Israeli settlements in the valley below.

The Syrian advance was initially slowed by an Israeli minefield and by deadly, accurate cannon fire. With dozens of Syrian tanks destroyed, the first few hours of the war were encouraging for the Israeli crewmen–their intense training was paying off. Knowing they would be outnumbered in any engagement, the Israeli tankers had trained relentlessly on gunnery skills and rapid target acquisition to ensure kills on the first shot. Undeterred by their losses, however, the Syrians kept coming, apparently convinced that, if worst came to worst, and the mass of their onslaught would ultimately overwhelm the defenders.

When fighter aircraft were called in to help stem the flow of Syrian armor, many of the Douglas A-4 Skyhawk's and McDonnell F-4E Phantoms that responded to the plea were shot down or damaged by the Syrians' dense anti-aircraft umbrella. Aware that Israeli doctrine relied on air power to even the score against the Syrian numerical advantage, the Syrians had acquired massive quantities of the latest Soviet missile and anti-aircraft systems. With the help of Soviet advisers, they created an air defense network over the Golan that was thicker than the one protecting Hanoi during the Vietnam War.

With their air support thus limited, the tankers were on their own–and the fate of northern Israel was in their hands. The Israeli tanks stood their ground and were knocked out one by one. Pushed beyond their limits, the defenses in the southern sector broke.

Bypassing the Israeli fortifications and pouring through gaps in the defenses, Syrian tanks pushed through the Israeli lines onto a wide-open plain that was ideal for tanks. The Israelis knew that they had to hold on at all costs to allow time for the reserves to mobilize, and in many cases the tank crews sacrificed themselves rather than give ground. As the hours passed, fewer and fewer Israeli tanks were left to stem the tide of oncoming tanks. The Syrian force split into a two-pronged advance.

Colonel Tewfik Jehani's 1st Armored Division moved northward toward the Golan command headquarters of Maj. Gen. Rafael Eitan, situated on the road leading down to the Bnot Yaakov Bridge, over the Jordan River and into the Israeli hinterland. The second prong of the Syrian attack, spearheaded by the 46th Armored Brigade of the 5th Infantry Division, moved south from Rafid on the southern access road toward El Al, with units breaking off toward the north in the direction of the Arik Bridge at the northern tip of the Sea of Galilee. Some 600 tanks were now engaged in the southern Golan, against which stood 12 tanks and isolated units that had been cut off near the various fortifications along the line.

Night offered no respite from the Syrian advance as they capitalized on their advantage of sophisticated night-vision equipment. The Israeli crews' long-distance firing efficiency was hampered by their lack of adequate night-fighting equipment. They did their best to overcome this obstacle by ordering illumination rounds to light up the sky, in conjunction with the xenon light projectors mounted on their tanks. Those were no match for the Syrians' infrared searchlights, so the Israelis did what they do best–improvise. They directed small tank units to carry out stopgap blocking actions against the far superior enemy forces–a tactic that may have prevented the Syrians from overrunning the entire Golan.

One of those lethal holding actions that have become legend was led by a young lieutenant named Zvi Gringold, affectionately known as 'Lieutenant Zvicka,' whose hit-and-run tactics are credited with single-handedly holding at bay a major thrust by almost 50 tanks. His guerrilla-style tactics on the route leading toward his brigade's HQ caused the Syrians to believe they were up against a sizable Israeli force. After more than ten of its tanks were destroyed, the Syrian column withdrew, its commander deciding to hold off and deal with the Israeli force in daylight. Gringold continued to engage the Syrians throughout the night and following day, destroying upward of thirty tanks, until injuries, burns and exhaustion caught up with him and he was evacuated. Gringold recovered and was subsequently awarded Israel's highest decoration, *Ot Hagvura*, for his heroic defense of Nafakh.

Another blocking force operating in the south, albeit attached to the 7th Brigade, was 'Force Tiger' under Captain Meir Zamir. Force Tiger's seven tanks were sent to block a column of some forty Syrian tanks that had broken through at Rafid and was heading north–a move that threatened to cut off and isolate the 7th Brigade. Force Tiger laid an ambush that succeeded in destroying half the Syrian tanks during the wee hours of the morning. When twenty tanks escaped, Zamir prepared a second ambush that succeeded in finishing off the Syrian battalion just after dawn the next morning.

Yet another Syrian thrust by two brigades was advancing rapidly on the southern access road in that wide-open sector and inexplicably stopped short in its tracks just before reaching El Al. While some of its units fanned off toward other objectives to the north, a large part of the Syrian force failed to press its advantage, a move that in effect meant that the Syrians just waited for the Israeli reserves to arrive and engage them. A number of theories abound as to why the Syrians would halt their advance in the midst of their momentum, including fear of an ambush on what certainly should have been a heavily defended route, lack of flexibility and initiative once their objectives had been achieved, overextended supply lines and the more far-fetched fear of an Israeli nuclear reprisal in that critical hour. Whatever the true reason, their lack of initiative at a critical moment robbed the Syrians of the chance to reach the Jordan River–and perhaps beyond–virtually unopposed.

In the morning, the Syrians pressed their attack yet again. The few remaining defenders of the Barak Brigade pleaded for air support, which again suffered heavy losses. Ironically, the Syrians helped solve the problem of foiling the anti-aircraft missile threat. After the Syrians fired rockets at Israeli civilian areas, the *Chel Ha'Avir* (Israel Defense Forces/Air Force, or IDF/AF) responded with reprisal attacks on Syrian infrastructure in Damascus and beyond. To defend against these attacks, the Syrians pulled back some of their missile batteries from the Golan front. Overall, it took the IDF/AF several days to develop tactics and gain experience in defeating Syrian air defense systems, and 27 Israeli aircraft were lost on the Golan front in ground-support missions, as well as scores of others suffering various degrees of damage.

On the morning of October 7, Minister of Defense Moshe Dayan toured the Golan front and recognized how critical the situation truly was. Not only were the access routes into the Golan threatened, but also the entire north of Israel. Grasping the very real prospect of a Syrian breakthrough into integral Israel, the minister of defense considered a retreat to a line just forward of the escarpment overlooking the Jordan Valley for a major defensive stand–in effect putting his forces' backs against a wall. Israel prepared to destroy the bridges over the Jordan River to prevent a Syrian breakthrough.

The Syrian 1st Armored Division was advancing up the route toward the Golan HQ at Nafakh. Colonel Yitzhak Ben-Shoham, the Barak Brigade's commander, realized his brigade was for all intents and purposes destroyed. He therefore organized and led a small group of surviving tanks in a holding action that slowed the Syrian advance on his HQ for several hours until he and the rest of the defenders were killed. With the brigade commander dead, no reserves in sight and two Syrian brigades advancing toward the Golan HQ–and with some units having bypassed the base on both flanks–the situation could only be described as grave. Lead elements of the Syrian brigades actually reached Nafakh and broke through the base's southern perimeter. One Syrian T-55 crashed into General Eitan's HQ, only to be knocked out by the last operational tank in Gringold's platoon.

At that point, Eitan evacuated his headquarters to an improvised location farther to the north. Those left to defend the base manned two trackless Centurions from the camp repair depot and fired bazookas in a final stand that knocked out several Syrian tanks until those last Israeli tanks were destroyed. The 188th Barak Brigade was no more.

The Syrians were poised to overrun the Golan headquarters at Nafakh and, seemingly, the entire Golan. That final stand, however, was enough to buy a few crucial additional minutes. While the Syrians paused to regroup after their final opposition had been neutralized, the first Israeli reserve units began reaching what had become the front lines. Finding Syrian tanks milling about their command headquarters, the Israelis immediately opened fire and attacked, dispersing the Syrians.

The arrival of the Israeli reservists spelled the beginning of the end for Syria. For both sides, the war had been about time—the Israelis doing all they could to buy time until their reserves arrived, and the Syrians racing against the clock to achieve their objectives before the Israeli mobilization. While many more bloody battles would take place, those first reserve units coming up the Golan and engaging the Syrians at Nafakh meant that the tide had turned.

The reservists found the Syrians enjoying nearly free reign in the Golan's southern sector. With Syrian tanks advancing along the routes down toward the Jordan River, the critical situation allowed no time to organize divisions and brigades. Instead, platoons and companies of tanks and other units were rushed off to battle as quickly as the forces could be mustered, at times being thrown in against Syrian battalions and even brigades. The fresh Israeli reserve units halted the near–and, in some cases, actual–retreat of what remained of their front-line forces and set about checking the Syrian advance. By midnight on day two of the war, the reserves had managed to stabilize what had been a disintegrating front–with the Syrians having penetrated to areas a mere ten-minute drive from the Jordan River and Sea of Galilee and to less than a kilometer from El Al on the southern access road.

Those gains had not come easily. In spite of their superior numbers, the Syrians' supply lines, extending great distances from their rear areas to points deep into the Golan, had been decimated by the Israeli defenders, and they could no longer replenish and support their forces. Convoys of supplies and reinforcements were under constant attack by the IDF/AF, as well as IDF armor and other ground forces, severely straining the Syrian advance. While the Syrians dug in to consolidate their gains, the Israelis went on the offensive.

Brigadier General Moshe Peled led a division up the Ein Gev road into the center of the southern sector while Maj. Gen. Dan Laner's division moved up the Yehudia road farther to the north–a parallel advance that boxed in the 1st Syrian Armored Division and effectively brought the Syrians' brief conquest to an end. The Syrians fought viciously to free themselves from that pincer movement. A major confrontation near Hushniya camp, which the Syrians had captured the previous night and turned into a forward supply base, ended with hundreds of wrecked, burning and smoldering Syrian tanks and armored vehicles and other vehicles littering the landscape.

By October 10, the Israelis had forced the Syrians back to the antebellum cease-fire line in the southern sector. Well aware of the strong Syrian defensive preparations in the south, Israel chose the northern Golan, with its more difficult, less-defended terrain, as the launching area for its counterattack into Syria itself. Among the units joining the counterattack was the reincarnated Barak Brigade. Since 90 percent of its original commanders had been killed or wounded, Barak's remnants were joined by replacements, reorganized and returned to fighting strength for the counteroffensive that penetrated deep into Syria–until a United Nations-sanctioned cease-fire came into effect on October 23, officially ending hostilities.

Although the war ended with Israeli forces on the move toward the Syrian capital, the Yom Kippur War–or Ramadan War, as it is known to the Arabs–shattered the myth of Israeli invincibility. The Syrians' success in maintaining the element of surprise and its forces' discipline in executing its attack helped that country regain much of the honor it had lost in the debacle of 1967. The victorious Israelis, on the other hand, had won a Pyrrhic victory. Horrible losses had been suffered, epitomized by the obliteration of the 188th Barak Brigade. While the war reaffirmed the Israeli defense doctrine of relying on the reserves' arrival within 24 hours to defeat a numerically superior enemy force, there was no time for celebration as the country buried the 2,222 soldiers who had paid the ultimate price for their country's survival and attended to its 7,251 wounded.

By Gary Rashba

Issac's brother was caught in the middle of this escalating attack and fierce fighting. He was shell shocked and ended up in a comma in the hospital in Haifa. His family didn't know where he was or what had happened to him. The news was devastating and together as a family prayer was made for Issac's brother. There is no pain like not knowing if your brother is dead or alive. The waiting to find him was almost unbearable. But prayer was constant for him.

When his brother was found and came out of the comma he became the Rabbi Issac's father had wanted Issac to be, and still is to this day. Issac was kept in Jerusalem and he has a piece of metal from a bomb that stopped one half of an inch from his leg. Isaac was finally allowed to go home.

Another war had ended and the mighty hand of God to save Israel once again intervened in miraculous ways.

One year after the Yom Kippur War, Issac was called up for thirty days to the Sinai Desert to the Suez Canal. They wanted him to help establish the base with stations for

57

gasoline. He had to use his own car. He filled his car up with gas before starting his journey across the desert. He drove five hours at night and could not see where the roads were because of the blowing sand.

Issac recalls the experience vividly. He states, "My gas gage was on empty. This was a very dangerous position to be in. If the Bedouin's saw you driving at night, especially at night, they would kill you to take the car. I was on empty and only God could have helped me. My auto took me to one foot outside of the Gate and security came and put gas in the car so I could drive through the gate to safety behind the gate! It was truly a miracle in my life!"

Issac realized the mighty hand of God protecting him and Israel. During this war over 300 Egyptian tanks were destroyed and Israel only lost 20! Again the world wondered how was this possible?

KOTEL

ISSAC

# CHAPTER SIX

# LOVE IS IN THE AIR...

ঙ৩৪৪

There comes a time in every young man's life when being alone is not an option. One day in 1979 Issac was outside his brother's coffee shop and saw a group singing with their hands raised coming down the street. A woman was walking along with them, so Issac asked her what was going on. She told him it was a group from Oklahoma and the woman's name, that everyone called her, was Mama Winnie. Issac invited them all in to give his brother more business. Mama Winnie came back later and talked to Issac and told him he needed help.

She didn't speak Hebrew and Issac didn't speak English so his brother translated for them. Issac insisted he didn't need help, but Mama Winnie insisted that he did. Later that week she came back with something for Issac and she hid it under her coat. Mama Winnie told Issac this is what he needed, what she had brought to him, hidden under her coat. It was the Brit Hadashah (New Testament or Covenant in Hebrew).

Issac said, "No way!" He explained in no uncertain terms he could not even touch it. But Mama Winnie was not going to give up. She kept insisting, so he finally took it. He came home and hid it because with his father being so Orthodox Issac knew his father would have killed Issac for having it in his possession. His father prayed every day that Issac would become a Rabbi. He would not have entertained this book in his home!

One night Issac couldn't sleep so he got the book out and started reading. It started with Yeshua, son of King David. Issac thought wait a minute what's King David doing here? He's my king! He also read that Yeshua said, "You can go into your closet to pray." Issac remembered something his grandfather Halali had told him. Issac's grandfather never went to synagogue and said to him, "You do not have to be with ten men in a minion to pray. You can pray to God in your room alone."

Later Mama Winnie came back to see Issac and told him her daughter and granddaughter were making Aliyah to Israel and would arrive in a few days. One morning he was at the coffee shop and saw Mama Winnie with a woman and little girl.

When Issac was a teenager he was in love with Elizabeth Taylor. He had written her a letter and sent his picture addressed to Hollywood, California. He never heard anything from Elizabeth Taylor, but right now at this very moment he was looking at a woman that he thought Mama Winnie had brought Elizabeth to him! She was beautiful. Mama Winnie introduced her daughter, Patricia, and her granddaughter, Natasha, to Issac and invited him for dinner. She invited him for dinner at her top floor apt. on Ben Yehuda St.

Patricia, the black haired Elizabeth Taylor look alike, made Aliyah to Israel December of "79." She was with her daughter, nine year old Natasha. She and Natasha became the first ones to become Israeli citizens January 1, 1980. They went to live in the Absorption Center (Mera-claus-klitah-tah) in Gilo.

This is where you live to adjust to the Israeli culture and to go to (Ulpon) the language school to learn Hebrew. Nine year old Natasha went straight into the public Hebrew schools and Pat and Issac began dating. After their first date, they went to a live show, Issac took Pat home and she said, "Keep in touch." He then went over to his friend's house who spoke English and told him, "That American women want you to touch them after the first date." His friend laughed and explained it was just an expression meaning 'to call again.' Issac said he was disappointed with that new understanding.

**Pat's Point Of View:**

When Pat's Mother took her two days after arriving in Israel to Issac's brother's coffee shop on Yaffa Street she saw Issac looking out at her. She noticed him noticing her! Something about his eyes grabbed Pat in the middle of her stomach. Issac says when he looked at her and she looked at him that was it! Still to this day, thirty-eight years later, Pat says she still gets butterflies when Issac comes home or looks at her. This was truly love at first sight!

Her Mother asked Issac to dinner and formally introduced Patricia and her granddaughter, Natasha to him. She served spaghetti with loads of sauce. She kept filling Issac's plate, but he almost choked trying to eat it all. She then invited him for New Years to a friend's house whose husband was a chef at the Jerusalem Plaza Hotel. It was this night that she introduced him to Dr. Bob Lindsey from Norman, OK. He had lived with his wife, Margaret in Israel for over forty years. He spoke Hebrew better than most Israelis.

Later, Dr. Lindsey would spend much time with Issac. He had so many questions. Dr. Lindsey was a pastor of the Narkis Congregation in Jerusalem, in The Church of All Nations. This church existed before Israel was even a state! Dr. Lindsey knew the tragedy of war. He had his leg blown off by a mine while saving a little Arab boy who wanted to come back to the Jewish side. He walks perfect and you would never know he has a wooden leg. Dr. Lindsey's son-in-law, Kenneth Mullican, wrote the book, *ONE FOOT IN HEAVEN*.

Issac and Pat dated for a little over one year and then they married. Although they didn't speak each other's native language they could understand and know they wanted to be together. Pat's twenty year old daughter, Kim was making Aliyah to Israel one year later. Kim came on her own Jewish rights and took citizenship at age twenty. So Issac got a home with four bedrooms. When they picked up her daughter Kim, at Ben Gurion airport, Pat asked her, on the way back to Jerusalem, "When did she start sounding like a hick when she spoke?" All of a sudden Pat heard her own voice play back in her ear and she sounded the same! It was their Okie accent from Oklahoma.

Pat went to work in reservations at the Jerusalem Plaza Hotel after arriving in Israel. After that she was asked to work in the book store in East Jerusalem across from the Damascus Gate, which paid much more. Kim went to work at the bookstore on the Jewish side and went to Ulpon for five months to learn Hebrew.

Mama Winnie had left back to America to take care of her mother, who had had a stroke, until she passed away. Issac was going to the Church of All Nations to Saturday Shabbat School. This was the very church his dad had told him,

"Don't walk over there," when they would walk to their synagogue. Issac wanted to share with his friends. So it became known that he now believed in Yeshua was the Messiah that his people were praying for. He paid a great price for his new beliefs. The builders and all the shop owners stopped giving him business.

One night Issac, Pat, Kim, and Natasha had one can of corn in the house to eat. They prayed and the doorbell rang. It was Issac's brother Ellie. He said, "Last week was your birthday Issac, so I decided to take you to the Hilton Hotel for a steak dinner." It was the best steak they had ever eaten. Pat was sure Issac appreciated it because when she first came to Israel she didn't know how to cook! She tried to find a cookbook written in English with Israeli recipes to cook, but couldn't find one. The salt was a larger grain and stronger. At first Pat ruined so much food, but Issac was very patient with her.

Issac and Pat would go to buy groceries at the Supersoel and Issac would go, "moo, moo or baa, baa" for the kind of meat he wanted since they still really didn't speak each other's language. Because they both knew the Bible they really learned each other's language sitting at the table with the Hebrew-English Bible and Dictionary. They both knew the Torah and Tanock and Issac had just read the "Brit Hadashah" (New Covenant). Issac showed up for dinner every night. There were no phones there then.

If Issac couldn't pick Pat up at her work at the bookstore on the Arabic side of Jerusalem, she would take the Arabic bus to the Jewish side to take a Jewish bus to where they lived. Right where she got off to get the Jewish bus was a deli. Pat saw they had among other things, stuffed cabbage rolls.

65

So she bought some and came home to put them in a pan in the oven. When Issac came to dinner that evening he ate and couldn't believe it. He kept saying they tasted just like his mother's. When he asked Pat how she made them he looked at her and she couldn't lie. He was looking at her face to face so she told him the truth about the deli.

Issac and Pat learned to communicate using the Bible and all kinds of ways at the moments when needed. It brought them closer and today they have been married for thirty-eight years! After Kim arrived and had taken five months of Hebrew, she started dating. Pat would go to bed, but Issac knew how young Israeli guys were and he would stay up until she was home and make sure everything was alright.

Issac was always very loving taking care of everyone he knew. They went many places where they could see where the stories from the Old and New Testaments took place. They always took both daughters and Pat's best friend that had emigrated from Oklahoma. They had a wonderful time getting to know each other. Also, Issac never proposed, but just took it for granted that Pat and he would get married. They got married one year after meeting each other. It was fate!

DR. BILLY GRAHAM AND DR. BOB
LINDSEY

MAMA WINNIE

# CHAPTER SEVEN

## BACK TO AMERICA

ം෦

As Isaac got stronger in his belief of the Messiah. He grew in Bible knowledge and history. Dr. Bob Lindsey mentored him and Isaac became a regular student and loved to study the New Testament. In his life he never imagined the day he met Mama Winnie at his brother's coffee shop what a life changing experience it would be for him.

In the New Testament Yeshua had twelve disciples that He personally instructed, lived with, and mentored. All twelve apostles loved Yeshua, but even they did not quite understand that He was Yeshua HaMessiah, the Son of God. It took time and experience to become "all in" believers.

Isaac came to know the Messiah in a similar manner. He was mentored by great scholars and people who had committed their lives to Yeshua and to His people in Israel. He studied and saw how the Old Covenant and the New Covenant were together to show people how God blessed, encouraged, and corrected his children, the Jewish people. As Issac studied King David and when he studied the genealogy of the Messiah he saw where the line to Yeshua was preserved through the Jewish people.

*Matthew 1 King James Version (KJV)*
*1 The book of the generation of Yeshua from Nazareth, the son of David, the son of Abraham.*

*2 Abraham begat Isaac; and Isaac begat Jacob; and Jacob begat Judas and his brethren;*

*3 And Judas begat Phares and Zara of Thamar; and Phares begat Esrom; and Esrom begat Aram;*

*4 And Aram begat Aminadab; and Aminadab begat Naasson; and Naasson begat Salmon;*

*5 And Salmon begat Booz of Rachab; and Booz begat Obed of Ruth; and Obed begat Jesse;*

*6 And Jesse begat David the king; and David the king begat Solomon of her that had been the wife of Urias;*

*7 And Solomon begat Roboam; and Roboam begat Abia; and Abia begat Asa;*

*8 And Asa begat Josaphat; and Josaphat begat Joram; and Joram begat Ozias;*

*9 And Ozias begat Joatham; and Joatham begat Achaz; and Achaz begat Ezekias;*

*10 And Ezekias begat Manasses; and Manasses begat Amon; and Amon begat Josias;*

*11 And Josias begat Jechonias and his brethren, about the time they were carried away to Babylon:*

*12 And after they were brought to Babylon, Jechonias begat Salathiel; and Salathiel begat Zorobabel;*

**13** *And Zorobabel begat Abiud; and Abiud begat Eliakim; and Eliakim begat Azor;*

**14** *And Azor begat Sadoc; and Sadoc begat Achim; and Achim begat Eliud;*

**15** *And Eliud begat Eleazar; and Eleazar begat Matthan; and Matthan begat Jacob;*

**16** *And Jacob begat Joseph the husband of Mary, of whom was born Yeshua, who is called Messiah.*

**17** *So all the generations from Abraham to David are fourteen generations; and from David until the carrying away into Babylon are fourteen generations; and from the carrying away into Babylon unto Yeshua are fourteen generations.*

**18** *Now the birth of Yeshua from Nazareth was on this wise: When as his mother Mary was espoused to Joseph, before they came together, she was found with child of the Rhua Hakodesh.*

**19** *Then Joseph her husband, being a just man, and not willing to make her a public example, was minded to put her away privily.*

**20** *But while he thought on these things, behold, the angel of the LORD appeared unto him in a dream, saying, Joseph, thou son of David, fear not to take unto thee Mary thy wife: for that which is conceived in her is of the Rhua Hakodesh.*

**21** *And she shall bring forth a son, and thou shalt call his name YESHUA: for he shall save his people from their sins.*

*22 Now all this was done, that it might be fulfilled which was spoken of the Lord by the prophet, saying,*

*23 Behold, a virgin shall be with child, and shall bring forth a son, and they shall call his name Emmanuel, which being interpreted is, God with us.*

*24 Then Joseph being raised from sleep did as the angel of the Lord had bidden him, and took unto him his wife:*

*25 And knew her not till she had brought forth her firstborn son: and he called his name YESHUA.*

**_King James Version_ (KJV)**
_Public Domain_

According to one scholarly estimate, the New Testament has more than 4,000 references to the Old Testament; thus the books of the Old Testament have been important for Christians, "permanently valuable" because they were "written under divine inspiration."


Written by Rev. Fred West    Sukkat Chaim

For two thousand years since the destruction of the temple in Jerusalem, the Christian Church has made herself the center and focus of all who follow and or worship Jesus. Our perception of Jesus and his life has been greatly altered through the dominating structure of the Church of Rome.

It was never God's desire for Jews and Gentiles to be separated but to be one in Messiah, thus two becoming "one new man" as Brother Paul so beautifully describe the true Church.

After the fall of the temple, Rome made it a priority for the Church to become less Jewish and more Roman. The Council of Nicea forbade all Jewish believers and Christians to keep Passover. The Jews and Christians were still observing and Rome stated, "You will not keep Passover as the Jews do, but you will keep Easter as we have since ancient times." Easter is the worship of Ashtoreth, the pagan sexual Goddess of ancient Bal worship.

Contrary to what many believe, the seven feasts that Israel kept were not their own conception, but in Leviticus 23, "These feasts are the Feasts of the Lord."

Also, the Shabbat was not Jewish, but a God thing and was instituted in the completion of Creation. There is more stated in the Ten Commandments about the Shabbat than any of the other commandments. It happened also to be the Church of Rome that changed the Sabbath to Sunday.

Many and most Jews today have a very dark view of Christendom. This view is justified in history through the persecution that Christians directed at them in the "Name of the Lord." The Holocaust was nothing new to Israel, they have been experiencing such events since the beginning of them becoming a people. A people chosen by God Himself.

I will now speak of the Son of God by his earthly name, Yeshua. His name is not English, Roman, or Greek, but it is a Hebrew name. Christians have always made it a mandatory requirement for Jews who receive Yeshua to put away their Judaism and become like them. When receiving Yeshua, Jews become fulfilled Jews. Brother Shaul (Paul) was witness of the hearing of thousands of Jews who had come to believe in Yeshua, who were zealous for Torah.

Take Note of These Facts:

1. Yeshua did not change the Sabbath to Sunday
2. Yeshua did not abolish Passover (Pesach)
3. Yeshua did not give us Easter
4. Yeshua did not give us the sacrament
5. Yeshua did not abolish the Feasts of the Lord
6. Yeshua did not do away with Tora (in the Hebrew mindset "fulfills" was to explain it in a right way e.g. Yeshua talking to the Pharisees, "You say this, but I say this."
7. Yeshua has nothing to do with Christmas. Christmas also has its roots in Paganism.

All of this has been incorporated into Christian worship and tradition by satanic influences designed to taint the wonderful inheritance Yeshua has for the true believers.

Without the Jews the Gentiles will be incomplete. Without the Gentiles the Jews will be incomplete. Yeshua was a Jew. Christians become less like Yeshua when they reject His heritage.

8. Yeshua was not a Christian.
9. Yeshua did not come to start a new religion.
10. Yeshua worshipped in the temple and taught in the synagogues.
11. Yeshua kept the Sabbath.
12. Yeshua kept His Feasts (Lev. 23).
13. Yeshua never denied his heritage.
14. Yeshua was born a Jew.
15. Yeshua lived as a Jew.
16. Yeshua died as a Jew.
17. Yeshua rose from the dead a Jew.

18. Yeshua will return as a Jew.
19. Yeshua will reign in Jerusalem, the city of the Great King where Elohim, our heavenly Father chose to put His name.

Remember our Father of Faith Abraham of whom it was said in Genesis 12:3, "I shall bless those who bless you and curse those who curse you."

Thank you, Issac and Pat, for bringing to us both blessing and completeness.

Issac and Pat attend Sukkat Chaim every Saturday on Shabbot. Issac does the Passover (Pesach) like he grew up in Israel at Sukkat Chaim in Locust Grove, Oklahoma.

The young generation in Israel today, they have questions too. They don't see the ending of the wars and they don't understand why. And the answer is Yeshua. "That is what we need to tell my people," Issac says. Issac shares and speaks on Israel and the wars. Issac's greatest expression is through his beautiful creative, iron art that he designs.

As Issac studied he came to understand, in his heart and soul, the love Yeshua had for the Jewish people. He knew like the twelve apostles who followed Yeshua for three years and come to learn who He was, Issac came to his new beliefs in the Messiah slowly, and with long considerations of scriptures and seeking to understand his new beliefs. Issac came to his belief that Yeshua was the Messiah that his people pray and look for daily, and was willing to give everything for his beliefs.

It wasn't easy and many people in the town realized Issac had changed. They began to ignore him, reject him, and stop coming to him for business. It was hard and became a tremendous financial hardship. It is hard for people to understand, even for the Christians. Isaac found himself in the middle of no man's land. What must be understood by all people is that while an individual Jew can accept Yeshua as the Messiah, they can and technically remain, Jewish! Isaac remained Jewish and loved his country, traditions, and family. He likes to express it as he became a completed Jew.

It was hard even for the Christians to understand when Constantine in 325 AD wanted to be separate from the Jewish people that believed Yeshua was their Messiah. Both were told that Jews who believed this were not Jewish anymore but now only Christian. No Jews were invited to the Nicean Council in 325AD. Yeshua HaMessiah was born Jewish and when he returns, He will still return as a Jewish son of Elohim. Issac knew that not only was he Jewish, but felt even more and complete as a Jew now. He remained Jewish with even more love for his country, traditions, and family.

The hardship of accepting the Messiah was terrible on the family. The business became non-existent and there was a great price to pay for his personal decisions. Pat and Isaac decided that they must leave their beloved land of Israel and they decided to go to Oklahoma City, Oklahoma, in America. Pat had family in Oklahoma City. As they packed up and came to America they saw quickly that life would be hard as many "Christians" would not accept them. With the Jews and some Christians not excepting them they felt they were in a dessert for the first couple of years.

It was a struggle. Pat went back to the mortgage business for income and Issac went to work for a clothing store and went to English school at night. It was hard starting over, but once again God put scholars in Isaac's life and continued to teach him like He had done in Israel. In Israel it was Dr. Brad Young and Dr. Lindsay as he came to know others here. It was hard starting over, but with Isaac's gift for iron works he began to create wonderful, creative works of art that began to sell and help the family's income grow.

As Pat and Issac settled in America and he realized it was now his duty and responsibility to care for his wife and children he often thought about his father. He began to realize why his father was so stern. He realized his father wanted the best for him and taught him scriptures and a holy lifestyle. Isaac knew he had to do what the scriptures said or his father would make sure he did! It was his father's faith and he stood in what he believed in, that Isaac could make the decisions he ultimately did through study and perseverance. Isaac remembered his father as a faithful, spiritual, and a remarkable man that had to endure hardships and still take care of his family. Something he did with great integrity and honor.

"I remembered how he carried me home when a motorcycle hit me and he never left my side." Issac knew he wanted to be a great man and love and care for his family too.

As Issac kept up with his iron works he began to get jobs to do custom staircases and balconies, this really put his name out to the public. As he decided to move to Tulsa, OK things for the betterment of their lives began to happen. The man who had Isaac do the balconies had a building and paid for all the tools for Isaac to start his own business. Later Issac and Pat paid him back and the business began to grow. As he began to do the custom staircases a magazine covered the staircase, Issac was designing, and did an article on Issac. Through several media channels Isaac got even better known for his beautiful creative art in iron.

## ISSAC'S DREAM

Yeshua came to Issac in a dream and Issac said it was the most real and clear he ever had. He went to sleep with a question to God on his mind. All of a sudden he was little and at the foot of the cross looking up crying. He had a dreidel in his hand. Then whoosh! Yeshua was down in front of him all in white and hugging him. He talked with him on Issac's question, then said, "What's that in your hand? What does the dreidel say?" Issac said, "It says 'ness gadol hiyah po!'" (A big miracle was here!)

Yeshua said, "You see you and I can see and feel a big miracle. Before I leave I'll come visit you again." Then Issac remembered what his father told him when they had to move outside the Old City that Issac would be back one day and will go through the Lion's Gate to take back Jerusalem, and in the "Six-Day War" a big miracle happened Issac was part of the recapturing of Jerusalem!. Then Yeshua appeared again later, hugged him and said, "See I'm fine."
They both had tears in their eyes and Yeshua said they were tears of happiness. He said, "Shalom, I'll be back again soon." He really is the Light of the world. Issac recounts they only spoke in Hebrew, but the understanding and message was very real and clear to him.

Pat and Issac came to America in hardship and learned that a new life was possible and would be filled with many opportunities. They understood it would be difficult, but they never doubted that Yeshua would be with them all the way.

ONE OF THE STAIRCASES ISSAC DESIGNED AND BUILT
COVERED BY MEDIA

ANOTHER OF ISSAC'S BEAUTIFUL DESIGNS

CHOSEN FOR THE COVER OF TULSA'S "HOUSE OF DREAMS"

ISSAC AND PATRICIA

# CHAPTER EIGHT

## THE MEDIA TELLS HIS INCREDIBLE STORY

ର୍ଶ୍ୟ

After ten years Issac started his Golden Gates Ironworks, LLC in Bixby, Oklahoma. Reverend George Shafer had given a shop to Issac, to lease, that he owned. Issac was there for four years. His craftsmanship was exceptional and it started to draw attention to him and the beautiful works in iron that he created. Then he moved to Sapulpa, Oklahoma. Issac was remembering the Presidential Gates in Israel and the honor that it was for him to serve his nation. Now he was bringing that creative talent to personal homeowners and his name was given great honor and respect.

The Bixby Bulletin ran two articles, about Issac and a local television station did three interviews or stories on Issac. The following information is taken from this article. The article and pictures were done by Judy Lambert for the Herald Newspaper.

"Issac Halali is an ironwork master craftsman and owns Golden Gate Ironworks LLC miles west of Sapulpa on Route 66. Although most of his work consists of staircases, gates, and larger projects, Halali loves to share his faith through his smaller iron artwork like these menorahs-candle holders with the name Jesus in English and in Hebrew, and one of his most unique is a combination of the Star of David and the symbol of the Fish."

Issac helped design the Iron Gate at the home of the Israeli President in the 1960s. As he progressed in his skills of iron he felt peace was missing from his life. "The journey which brought him from his birthplace of Jerusalem, to Oklahoma was in itself an adventure.

With many wars that have gone on in and around Israel throughout history, Halali said he tried to build his ironworks business between the wars." One day he bridged the gap between Judaism and Christianity, when he accepted Yeshua as the Messiah. "I am now a completed Jew," he said. Growing up surrounded by wars and experiencing, first hand, the supernatural protection of Israel by the hand of the Almighty God, Halali knew that Israel was "God's People." He always knew there was something missing, and when he found that something in Yeshua, it was his desire to live to tell the truth of their Messiah who had come, not only for the Jew, but for the world.

"When people ask me about my faith, I just tell them I'm completed." Though many would call him a Messianic Jew, Halali said that he believes a little differently than most Messianic Jews. "This (the Messiah) is not only for the Jews. To me we (Jews and Christians) are in the same place. We have only one God, the Son of God, and the Holy Spirit. If we put it all together, we will be strong in the world to spread the good news. In the New Testament it is all about love; love your enemies, the main thing is to love."

"The young generation in this world today, have questions and disappointments. They don't have the understanding to help all the issues of pain and heartache people are enduring. They don't understand why, and the answer is Yeshua. That is what we need to tell my people."

84

Issac shares his testimony with others and with churches, but his greatest testimony is through the beautiful, creative, iron art that he designs. The following pictures are of some of the jobs and artwork Issac has created.

Many newspapers began to showcase Issac, his story, and incredible iron works. Some of the media Issac was showcased in are:
*Builder/Architect the Art of Architecture*
*Tulsa Street or Dreams, 2005,* Issac's staircase was the cover of the Magazine.
*The Tulsa World*
*The Bulletin, Retheriod Publications, Inc.* and many more.
*Sapulpa Daily Herald*
*TBN (Christian television station)*

Issac was very fortunate to have television interested in his testimony and in May of 2017 Issac was on 'The Deborah Sweetin Ministries' television show again to speak about The Six-Day War, and what it was like to take back the Old City of Jerusalem after 2,000 years.

Steve Tremble was with Pat and Issac watching the television interview show being taped. Issac shared how his heart was yearning to be there in Jerusalem on June 5th for this 50th Jubilee celebration of the Six-Day War. A few days later Steve surprised Issac when he showed up with two tickets for himself and Issac. Issac was so appreciative, he was going to be there! He was really going to be in Jerusalem for the celebration.

Issac and Steve left at the end of May for over three weeks. In Jerusalem there were so many people, because

85

President Trump was there also. They couldn't find parking by their place they were to stay at, so they knew they were going to carry all their luggage a long way to the hotel. Issac didn't know how he was going to be able to do this, when all of a sudden he looked up and there was Robert Easton, his close friend from Tulsa. He seemed to always be there for Issac and Pat in Tulsa, and now here he was in Jerusalem picking up Issac's luggage to carry for him. Robert sings and plays the harp wherever Issac and Pat go, and this was just a beautiful blessing at this time in Isaac's life. The next day Issac was with 100's of others on the streets of Jerusalem!

Starting at the Bat Sheba Hotel where Pat and Issac stayed when they married, Issac danced on King George St. to where Jaffe St., King George St. and Ben Yehuda St. meet together. When Issac was too tired to move, he went back to their hotel room to rest and called Pat with tears running down his cheeks to tell her how happy and blessed he was feeling. It was a tremendous day for Issac and a memory he will never forget.

Israel had a month of shows and celebrations. Especially in Jerusalem. Jerusalem Day happened to be at this time also. Every night they ate at one of Issac's sisters or brothers homes or they took them to a nice restaurant. It was a very joyous time for Issac. "Jerusalem, oh Jerusalem how I love you."

ISSAC AT THE WESTERN WALL "KOTEL"

ISSAC AND PATRICIA

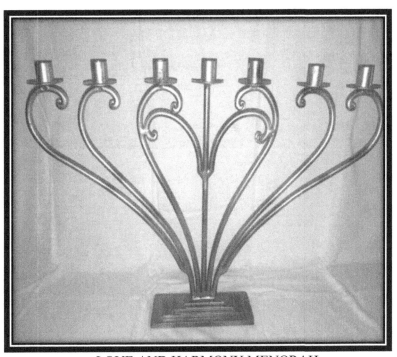

LOVE AND HARMONY MENORAH
24" WIDE X 20" HIGH

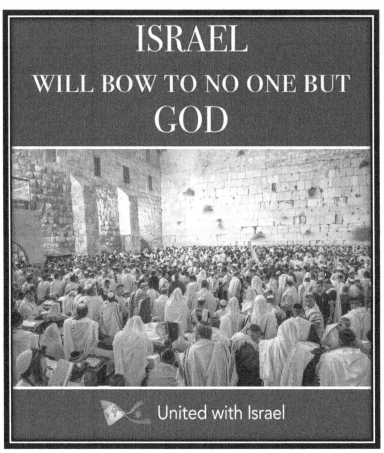

ISRAEL
WILL BOW TO NO ONE BUT
GOD

United with Israel

KOTEL

# CHAPTER NINE

# FAMILY
## THE CORD THAT BINDS LOVE TOGETHER

೮೦೦೮

Trials and tribulations, joys, laughter, tears, and security are just some of the wonderful experiences that happen in a loving and tight knit family. Issac is well aware that his family is a gift from God. With nine brothers and sisters something was always going on. Issac's mom had ten living children and two that had died. With that many children it was no surprise that Issac and Saul slept on the roof!

For Issac's 80$^{th}$ birthday his sisters and Issac's brothers threw him a birthday party in Jerusalem. Issac is very proud of all his brothers and sisters and loves them all. His brothers and sisters met at a very nice restaurant to celebrate and throw an 80$^{th}$ surprise birthday party for Issac.

This was one of the happiest family moments for Issac and Pat. It was a night of beautiful fellowship, fun, respect, and overflowing love. The family was a strong force when they joined together in unity. Issac recounts the story of when the whole family prayed for the life of his brother, and together they saw a miracle. He came out of his comma and became the Rabbi that Issac's father desired him to be. Today, he still serves Israel as a great man of God, Rabbi Halali.

Issac remembers when he was little and he and his father were coming back from the synagogue in the Old City and all of a sudden a group of Arabs surrounded them and were saying really bad things. Just as they were going to attack them, three Israelis appeared and saved them. He said he thought it was the Hagana. This was a group that secretly fought to defend Israelis and later became the Israeli military after 1948.

Also this reminded Issac of when they first moved to Tulsa. Issac was outside by his car on the street and a man appeared and said to him God wants you to drive a better car than this. Pat saw this from the window and went out to see if Issac was understanding what the man was telling him. The man was walking down the middle of the street and as they were looking he just disappeared. Pat recalled how her mom always told her that a car represents your way of life in a dream. Family and family connections were a very important part of Issac's and Pat's life, both in America and Israel.

From Issac's own words he says, "Let me tell you just a little about my brothers and sisters.

Ester passed in the night from the flu in 2016 suddenly. When my parents became older Ester came every Thursday and cleaned and cooked for Shabbat for them, along with Mazel. Mazel and Ester were twins. Ester's husband, Avi, is Chief of Police.

Guela her name means *Redemption*, is probably the most loving person someone could ever know. All of the siblings are loving, but Guela has something special in this gift. Her husband Zvika is also a Police career and at one time Guela was also Police, and her daughter and her husband are also in police careers.

Elijah who was always called Ellie, meaning *Belonging to God.* He was always starting businesses and had many. He owns women's dress stores at this time and his wife and mother of his children died of brain cancer. He married and Sima has now been with him for over sixteen years. Sima is a very smart woman and speaks many different languages. More open than all the family Ellie's the one brother that lives in KAFAR TAVOR. You can look up and see the top of Mt. Tavor. He told me he would take me there since "What's his name went to heaven from there!" He would not say the word, Yeshua. He finally did when we were up there and I was telling him with Sima it would not kill him to say Yeshua. As brothers we are extremely close.

"Elli is the brother that I carried on my back every day to Hadassah Hospital for them to work on his crooked feet that he was born with. I carried him because he could not walk the distance and I loved him and wanted him to get better. His feet are fine now. They would not give Ellie a driver's license in Israel because of his eyes, so he and his first wife decided to go to America because of her brain cancer and they hoped for specific health care for them. We had a friend Dr. Conner who had Ellie's eyes operated on. Pat's mother, Momma Winnie was back in America from Israel on a trip to check on everyone and she taught Ellie how to drive in front of mine and Pat's house. We would look out the window and there they would go Ellie and Mama Winnie going back and forth. They finally gave him a license here to drive certain hours of the day."

Shibolet's name means *Oats* and she is giving and caring to everyone. Her husband Manashem and his brothers did most of the roads in Israel until we all became older.

Shaul means *Borrowed* and he is a graphologist. The government uses him when important people come to Israel to read their handwriting to see if they are honest and to understand their character traits. His wife is Piola, from Brazil, and use to teach English.

Rena means *Happy* and she is the oldest daughter. At age seven she started helping mother raise the children, feeding them etc. Her husband Itchak is an Arkia Airlines Pilot.

Mazel *(luck)* helped Ester with 'doing for' our older parents for Shabbat. Her husband became the best at ironwork after Issac left. He does ironwork for the new Malls and Skylights.

Yudit *(femine) (Tribe of Judah)* She married a Hasidic Jew and they are still in Israel today.

Yuda *(masculine)* is my youngest brother and was not very religious until the Yom Kippur War. Only eighteen and in the military for the first time and only a few weeks when he was removed from the battles and placed in the hospital in a comma. He was sent to the Golan Heights up north and I was sent to Sini down South. They contacted me and let me know that my brother was in the hospital in Hifa and in a comma. Yuda could not take the atrocities he saw. The brothers and sisters kept up prayer for Yuda and eventually he came out of the coma. He studied and became the Rabbi Issac's father always wanted Issac to be!

94

So that is just a little bit of information I wanted to share about my siblings. Family makes you strong, encourages you, laughs, and cries with you and most of all loves you. In Israel the absolute need to have strong loving families is essential. Life can be hard and wars pull at you emotionally. We didn't have a lot, but we had parents who loved us and we loved each other. That is a tremendous blessing from God."

This surprise birthday party in Jerusalem was bringing a flood of memories and filling Issac's heart to overflowing. To turn 80 in Jerusalem with your family, who could ask for anything more? Reviel's (granddaughter's) cake (pictured below) was for her Bat Mitzvah, but since Issac had bombs dropping when it was his Bar Mitzvah he claimed it for his 80th birthday cake. She wanted Our God is One on it. So it worked for Issac too. After she gave her speech Issac stepped up to the microphone and gave his also. They are inseparable. Tallia was born nine months later and she is also very close to Issac and Pat. Issac loves them very much and they have lived with him for ten years now.

REVIEL'S BAT-MITZVAH CAKE. SHE ASKED FOR
THE WORDS ON IT. ISSAC HER "SABA"
(GRANDFATHER IN HEBREW) ENJOYED IT FOR HIS
BAR-MITZVAH ALSO!

ISSAC AND REVIEL

ISSAC

# CHAPTER TEN

## BECOMING AN AMERICAN CITIZEN

୫୦୦୪

After arriving in America it became apparent that life would not be so easy. One of the biggest problems Issac would have was learning to speak English in a way that he felt confident in. Pat helped, but as Issac went to churches to share his testimony it became apparent he would have to get much better in his communication skills. Not speaking the language made it difficult to find jobs too.

One of the first jobs Issac took was working in a women's department store and he being a man in the store was a little awkward. It ended when he was celebrating his birthday that they were throwing him and dancing with a belly dancer! Eventually, Issac met an Israeli man who purchased some apartment buildings that needed rehabbed and he hired Issac to do the work. He supplied the place for Issac to work out of and he supplied all the tools and equipment Issac needed to do this job. Issac worked on these projects three years.

The man who had so blessed Issac now wanted Issac to build balconies on the second floor and up. Issac was able to show his talent and many calls started coming in for staircases, gates, and other architectural designs. This was a tremendous time for Pat and Issac as they began to finally see success in America.

Issac decided to become an American citizen. His heart still belonged to Israel, but he also wanted to be an American citizen. His biggest dream was to be able to vote and after he got his citizenship he immediately registered to vote. Issac has dual citizenship in Israel and in America. That means two passports and he was happy he could keep his Israel citizenship also.

In order to learn English better Issac went to a school to get the help he needed. He studied hard and today speaks English fairly well. Issac's family in Israel were happy for him and supported his American lifestyle. As Pat and Issac reflected on the history of Israel and the past they realized they were in a divine plan of Yahweh.

As Queen Isabella wrote the edict to expel the Jews in 1492 from Spain, Issac's mother's family would be part of that exodus, and her family would go to Israel. In May of 1948 Isaac's family was right in the middle of the declaration to create Israel as a nation! This was a historical moment, but greater still it was a prophetic moment fulfilling the scriptures. A miracle moment!

The world looked on in absolute wonder as Yahweh fulfilled His word to allow the Jews to return to Israel. Part of the declaration read, "The state of Israel will be open to the immigration of Jews from all countries of their dispersion; will promote development of the country for the benefit of all its inhabitants; will be based on the precepts of liberty, justice, and peace taught by the Hebrew Prophets; will uphold the full social and political equality of all its citizens, without distinction of race, creed or sex; will guarantee full freedom of conscience, worship, education and culture; will safeguard the sanctity and inviolability of the shrines and Holy Places of all religions; and will dedicate itself to the principles of the Charter of the United Nations."

A divine moment in history and Issac again found himself in the middle of a miracle! Again, Issac realized he was there chosen by God to be present in God's purpose and plans. Moment's history will never forget, the Jewish people can never deny, and the believers in Yeshua can remain hopeful in.

The well-known Pastor Adrian Rogers wrote this about Israel. "I want help in understanding the present and the future, because there is Bible prophecy yet to be fulfilled (now fulfilled)! Keep your eyes on Zion, God's holy land. As the Jew goes so goes the world. The Jews are God's yardstick, God's outline, God's blueprint, for what He's up to in the rest of the world. The land of Israel, I believe is the most important spot on earth. The most important city is not Washington or Moscow, but Jerusalem. The most important land, is not America but tiny Israel, about the size of New Jersey."

1. The land of Israel always has God's eyes watching them Deuteronomy 11:12.
2. God promised to return the people and rebuild the desolate cities Amos 9:14.
3. God is always present in Israel Genesis 28:16.
4. A land filled with joy and peace II Chronicles 23:21.
5. God promises to protect Jerusalem Isaiah 31:5.
6. God will establish His salvation in Zion Isaiah 46:13.
7. Jerusalem will be a source of praise Isaiah 62:7.

Israel as a nation and fulfillment of prophetic scriptures happened in 1948. The declaration ends, "With trust in Almighty God, we set our hand to this Declaration, at this session of the Provisional State Council, in the city of Tel Aviv, on this Sabbath eve, the fifth of Iyar, 5708, the fourteenth day of May, 1948." As Issac was soon to learn trust in Almighty God can be a journey in life that brings life great meaning and purpose.

As he recalled the Flag of Israel he was reminded of how prayer plays an important role in Israel's history. "We have a flag and it is blue and white. The *tallit* (prayer-shawl) which we wrap ourselves in when we pray: has become our symbol. "Let us take this *tallit* from its bag and unroll it before the eyes of Israel and the eyes of all nations. So a blue and white flag with the Shield of David painted upon it was ordered. That is how our national flag that flew over Congress Hall came into being. And no one expressed any surprise or asked whence it came, or how."

It seems that Issac's journey through life has travelled the road to Israel's fulfilled promises from Yahweh. As Issac took his oath to become an American citizen he had great pride, but he also recalled the National Anthem of the State of Israel, the words came fresh to his mind,

"So long as still within our breasts
The Jewish heart beats true,
So long as still towards the East,
To Zion, looks the Jew.
So long our hopes are not yet lost-
Two thousand years we cherished them-
To live in freedom in the Land
Of Zion and Jerusalem."

As Issac reflected on his citizenship in America he couldn't help but remember Israel. He was blessed with the best in both worlds. Almighty God had blessed him and his family with freedom few in the world ever experience. The freedom of America and the freedom of Israel. Issac promised himself that one day he would return to Israel.

Issac went back to visit Israel on his 80$^{th}$ birthday. He says, "I want to build the relationship between the Jewish people and America. This is what I want to share. It is important to me! I MUST LET MY PEOPLE KNOW!"

# CHAPTER ELEVEN

## ISSAC AND PAT: FUTURE PLANS

☙℞

Issac and Pat have been married for 38 years and work together in the Kingdom of God and reside in Tulsa, OK. Issac does his creative iron art work and is very well known internationally. It is their great desire to return back to Israel to live and work for the rest of their lives. Pat and Issac now believe that it is time to return to their homeland of Israel. They have lived in America for over thirty years.

Many of the following pictures are of Issac's creative artwork.
The following picture is a custom cross and Menorah that was designed for Hallelujah Women's Ministry.

*Hallelujah Women and now also Hallelujah Men are in several states. God showed Cynthia Ward to come to Oklahoma City, to begin to do the same here and she was joined to Louise and Byron Amick in this endeavor. Much prayer and fasting go into having these meetings. We all meet every three months at this time in a Lodge in Anadarko, OK. This is for prayer with praise and worship along with different anointed speakers. Robert Easton along with Issac and Pat travel from Tulsa to Anadarko looking forward to these times.

Issac and Pat wanted to end this book in a special way with the Birkat Kohanim Blessing. This is the Priestly blessing and an ancient benediction. Today, it is recited in the synagogues as the only prayer God said to pray from Him! In the Jewish community this is the most important prayer. The people wash their hands, remove their shoes, cover their heads with the tallit and raise their hands in the shape of the Hebrew letter "Shin" to prepare for the blessing. We would like to share the full Hebrew Meaning. Numbers 6:24-26 KJV http://bible.com/1/num.6.24-26.kjv
(This exert was taken from Sid Roth's television show).

KOHANIM BLESSING

THE LORD BLESS YOU...
May YHWH (He who exists) kneel before you (making Himself available to you as your Heavenly Father) so He can bestow upon you, His promises and gifts.

AND KEEP YOU...
And guard you with a Hedge of Thorny Protection that will prevent Satan and all your enemies from harming you. May He protect your body, soul, mind and spirit, your loved ones and all your possessions.

THE LORD MAKE HIS FACE SHINE UPON YOU...
May YHWH (He who exists) illuminate the wholeness of His being toward you, continually bringing to you order so you will fulfill your God given destiny and purpose.

AND BE GRACIOUS TO YOU...
May YHWH (He who exists) provide you with perfect love and fellowship (never leaving you) and give you sustenance (provision) and friendship.

THE LORD LIFT HIS COUNTENANCE ON YOU...
May YHWH (He who exists) lift up and carry His fullness of
being around you (bringing everything that He has for you.

AND GIVE YOU PEACE...
And may YoHoVah YHWH your Heavenly Father set in place
all your needs to be whole and complete so you can walk in
victory moment by moment by the power of the Holy Spirit.
May He give you supernatural peace welfare, safety,
soundness, tranquility, prosperity, perfection, fullness, rest,
harmony, as well as the absence of agitation and discord.
Amen.

*We bless you in Yeshua's name because He is our high priest now!*

KOHANIM BLESSING

ISSAC AFTER OFFERING THE KOHANIM BLESSING

# THE VISION

The vision and cry of our hearts is to "LET MY PEOPLE KNOW" about Yesuha HaMeshia and to experience the love and forgiveness He gives to us. He paid the price for us to have the happiness, joy, and anointing of the Ruach HaKodesh (Holy Spirit) that is ours to have. To know we have Him every moment through all our ups and downs in life. To have His grace put a cloak around us, no matter what happens or what it seems we're going through. To have the Holy Spirit lead and guide us in all we face or need, no matter what happens or what the situation is. To be able to experience and know He will never leave us nor forsake us. He is our Healer and Provider and in Him we trust. He guides us in our decisions as long as we allow Him too. We can keep such a confidence and such a joy in this life, no matter what turmoil this world is in and know we are in the palms of His hand. Until that day when we are in heaven we will praise Him and pray to accomplish what our Heavenly Father has put us on this earth to accomplish. Also, He has put you here for a specific reason for you to accomplish.

Let us praise our Heavenly Father for all He has done and is doing, to bring the Christian and Jew together. On both sides we have been lied to. On the Christian side, they were told the Feasts were Jewish feasts, instead of our Heavenly Father's feasts. On the Jewish side we were told if we believed Yeshua was the Messiah, then we were Christians and no longer Jewish. This is far from what He intended for us on this earth.

May we show His love and forgiveness to our loved ones and the ones he put in our paths, to bring the Christian and Jew together as our Heavenly Father originally intended us to be, "The One New Man."

This is what we live for so we pray, "LET MY PEOPLE KNOW!"
Issac and Patricia Halali

ISSAC AND PATRICIA

# HOW TO ORDER OR GET IN TOUCH WITH ISSAC AND PATRICIA HALALI

EMAIL: Halali@sbcglobal.net

The following pictures are just some of the creative ironwork of internationally known artist Issac Halali.

If you need to contact Issac or Pat for more information please use the email address given above.

If you would like a custom designed piece notify Issac for interview times and discussions.

Issac does many custom designs for churches, corporations, and private collections.

For speaking invitations just email or leave a telephone number for return contact. Leave a brief message and information of what your specific need is and Issac and Patricia will get back with you.

Facebook: Issac Halali Artisan

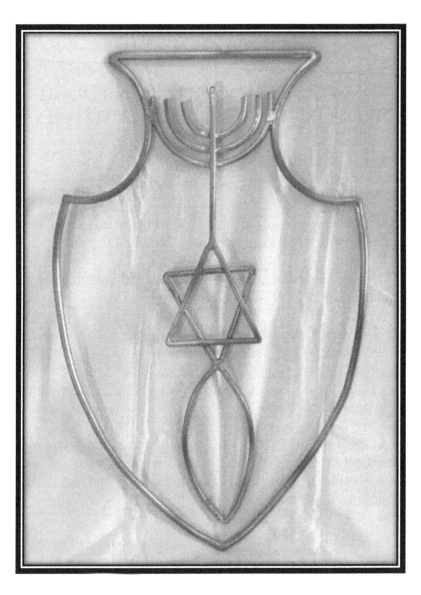

ONE NEW MAN IN SHIELD OF FAITH
18" HIGH X 12" WIDE
GRAFTED IN CHRISTIAN AND JEW

114

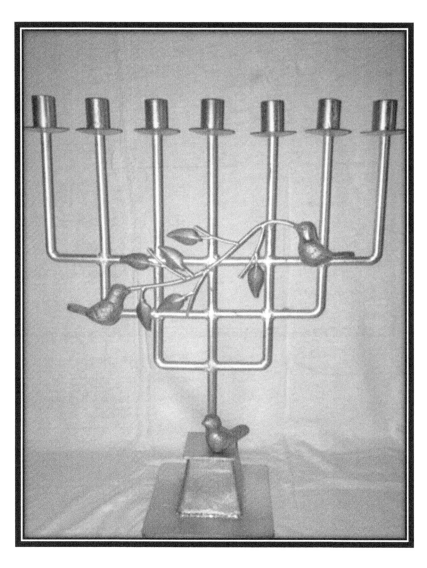

DOVES WITH OLIVE BRANCH
20" HIGH X 18" WIDE

115

1700 AD MENORAH 21" HIGH X 17" WIDE

TORAH TEN COMMANDMENTS MENORAH 16" WIDE X 18"
HIGH

BURNING BUSH
18" WIDE X 20" HIGH "LET MY PEOPLE GO" IN
HEBREW

ONE NEW MAN WITH GRAPE LEAF
JEW AND CHRISTIAN TOGETHER
16" WIDE X 24" HIGH

100 AD MENORAH

FOUND ON THE FLOOR OF 100 AD SYNAGOGUE
18 "WIDE X 23" HIGH

STAR OF DAVID MENORAH WITH
GRAPE LEAVES

20" HIGH X 16" WIDE

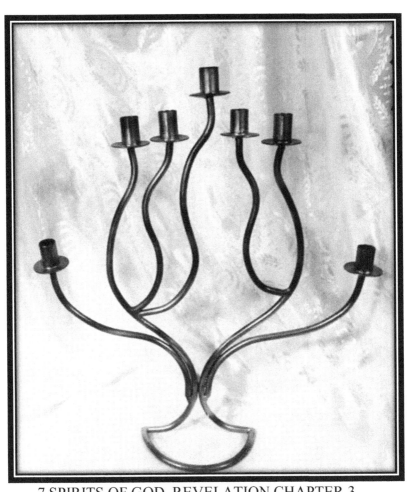

7 SPIRITS OF GOD  REVELATION CHAPTER 3
19" WIDE X 22" HIGH

HANUKKEA FOR HANUKKA
20" WIDE X 16" HIGH

**SHABBAT LIGHTS MENORAH**
**14" WIDE X 12" HIGH**
CANDLES SEPARATE

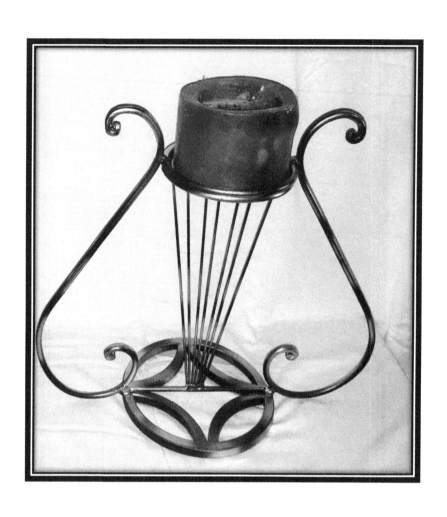

KING DAVID'S HARP
2 SIZES
SMALL 12" WIDE X 12" HIGH
LARGE 22" WIDE X 14" HIGH

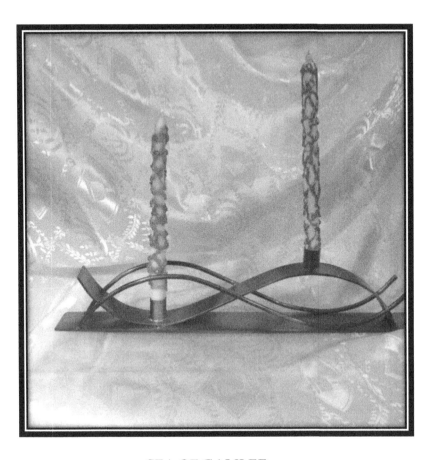

SEA OF GALILEE
41/2" HIGH X 20" WIDE
CANDLES SEPARATE

HALLELUJAH IN HEBREW
20" WIDE X 3 ½ "HIGH
CANDLES SEPARATE

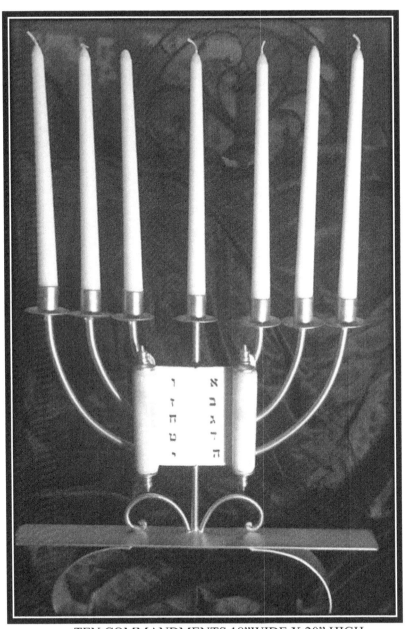

TEN COMMANDMENTS 18"WIDE X 20" HIGH

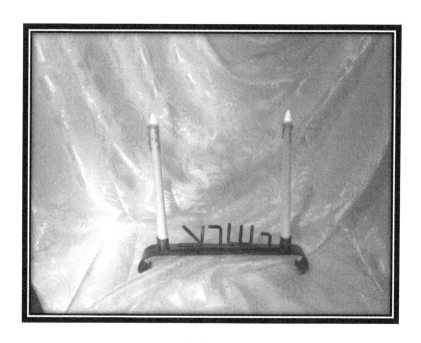

YESHUA
14" WIDE X 3 1/2 "HIGH

3' WIDE 5' HIGH

Vision of Steve Tremble

70 LEAVES REPRESENTS 70 JUDGES OF THE SANHEDRIN
WAVES: REPRESENT SEA OF GALILEE
TRUNK AND ROOTS: REPRESENT OLD TESTAMENT
BRANCHES: REPRESENTS THE JEWISH
FULLNESS OF THE TREE:  GRACE OF NEW TESTAMENT

PRAY FOR THE PEACE OF JERUSALEM

# NOTES

24371330R00076

Made in the USA
Middletown, DE
22 December 2018